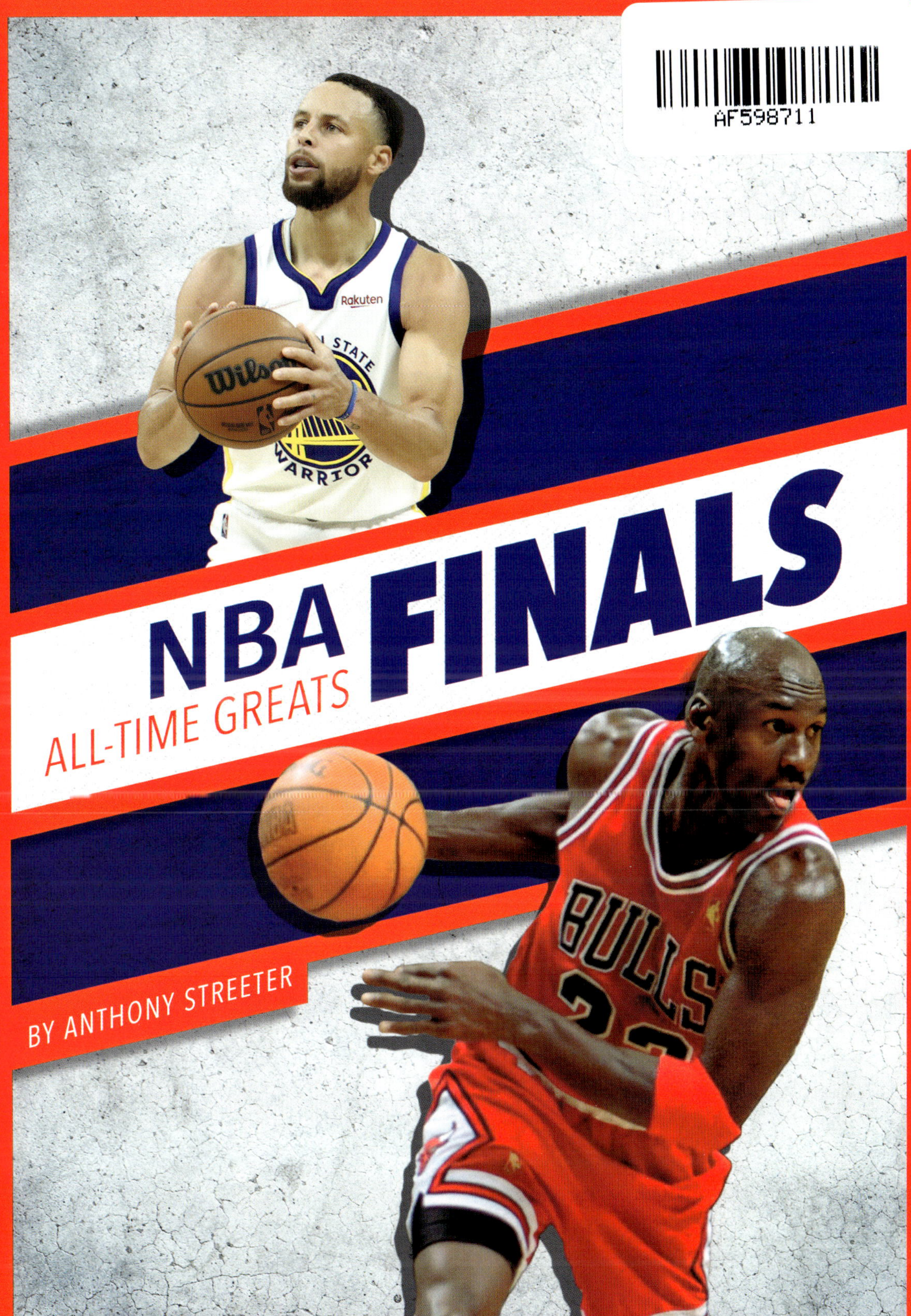

NBA FINALS

ALL-TIME GREATS

BY ANTHONY STREETER

Book design by Jake Slavik
Cover design by Jake Slavik

Photographs ©: Jed Jacobsohn/AP Images, cover (top), 1 (top); Winslow Townson/AP Images, cover (bottom), 1 (bottom); Bettmann/Getty Images, 4, 10; TPLP/Archive Photos/Getty Images, 7; Rick Stewart/Allsport/Hulton Archive/Getty Images, 9; Christian Petersen/Getty Images Sport/Getty Images, 13; Jed Jacobsohn/Getty Images Sport/Getty Images, 15; Ronald Martinez/Getty Images Sport/Getty Images, 16; Ezra Shaw/Getty Images Sport/Getty Images, 19; Jonathan Daniel/Getty Images Sport/Getty Images, 21

Press Box Books, an imprint of Press Room Editions.

ISBN
978-1-63494-862-3 (library bound)
978-1-63494-880-7 (paperback)
978-1-63494-915-6 (epub)
978-1-63494-898-2 (hosted ebook)

Library of Congress Control Number: 2023923230

Distributed by North Star Editions, Inc.
2297 Waters Drive
Mendota Heights, MN 55120
www.northstareditions.com

Printed in the United States of America
082024

ABOUT THE AUTHOR

Anthony Streeter is a former sportswriter who has written for various newspapers. He lives in Columbia, Missouri, with his wife and three kids.

TABLE OF CONTENTS

RUSSELL
6
CELTICS
6
BOSTON
CELTICS
1960
EASTERN DIV
CHAMPIONS

CHAPTER 1 EARLY ICONS

The first National Basketball Association (NBA) Finals took place in 1947. By 1949, **George Mikan** started to dominate the series almost every year. At 6-foot-10 (208 cm), Mikan towered over opponents. Nobody played like him in the early days of the NBA. Mikan sunk hook shots from the post. Rebounds seemed to stick to his hands. By 1954, the star center had led the Minneapolis Lakers to five championships.

No player won more titles than **Bill Russell**, though. The powerful center anchored the NBA's greatest dynasty.

Starting in 1957, his Boston Celtics won 11 championships in 13 years. Russell served as player-coach for the last two. Russell wasn't flashy on the court. He simply dominated, especially on defense. Other stars helped as well. Swingman **John Havlicek** never lost in eight trips to the Finals. Two of those wins came after Russell retired.

Only one team beat Russell and the Celtics in the Finals. Forward **Bob Pettit** made sure of it. His St. Louis Hawks met the Celtics four times in the Finals. In Game 6 of the 1958 series, Pettit scored 50 points. At the time, no player had

STAT SPOTLIGHT

NBA FINALS RECORD

CAREER REBOUNDS

Bill Russell: 1,718

scored more in a Finals game. Pettit's late tip-in secured the championship for the Hawks.

The New York Knicks appeared to be in trouble in the 1970 Finals. Star center **Willis Reed** tore his thigh muscle. He missed Game 6. No one knew if he would appear in

Game 7. Reed played through the pain, though. He came out and hit two early jumpers. His inspired teammates went on to win. Three years later, a healthy Reed led New York to another championship. He earned Finals Most Valuable Player (MVP) honors both times.

Center **Kareem Abdul-Jabbar** led the Milwaukee Bucks to the 1971 championship in his second NBA season. But he's best known for his time with the Los Angeles Lakers. Abdul-Jabbar destroyed opponents with his hook shot. Meanwhile, point guard

GREAT EFFORT

Guard Jerry West led the Los Angeles Lakers to nine NBA Finals. In those games, he scored a record 1,679 points. However, his only title came in 1972. Six losses came against Bill Russell and the Celtics. In a 1969 loss, West was so good he earned Finals MVP honors. No other losing player has won the award.

Magic Johnson ran the Lakers' offense. Their exciting teams were nicknamed "Showtime." Together, they reached eight Finals and won five.

The Lakers had a heated rivalry with the Celtics in the 1980s. Los Angeles beat Boston in the Finals twice during that era. But versatile forward **Larry Bird** led the Celtics past the Lakers in 1984. The Celtics won three titles in the 1980s. Bird earned Finals MVP honors in two of them.

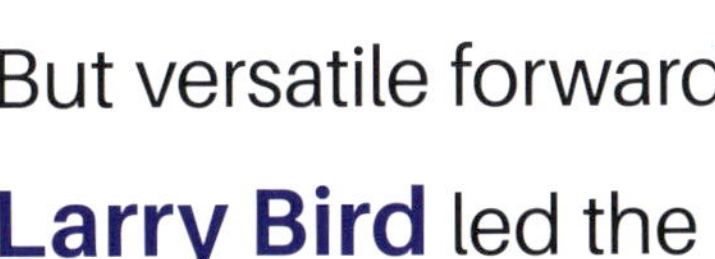

JORDAN
23

CHAPTER 2

NEXT-LEVEL STARS

No team had an easy time against the Detroit Pistons in the late 1980s. The bruising squad was nicknamed the "Bad Boys." The name described **Isiah Thomas** perfectly. The point guard played with a hard edge on the court. Behind his toughness, Detroit won the 1989 and 1990 championships.

Michael Jordan and the Chicago Bulls fell to Detroit in the playoffs both years. But the Bulls finally got past the Pistons in 1991. Then Chicago became unstoppable. Jordan played with a fierce mentality. The shooting guard seemed to score at will. And he played lockdown defense as well. Having **Scottie Pippen** as a sidekick helped, too. The forward could shut down an opponent's best scorer. Together, Jordan and Pippen led Chicago to six NBA Finals from 1991 to 1998. The Bulls won all six. Jordan was the Finals MVP and leading scorer each time.

The Bulls might have won even more titles. However, Jordan briefly retired in 1993. That opened the door for **Hakeem Olajuwon**. The 7-foot (213 cm) center overpowered opponents on offense and defense. And his

STAT SPOTLIGHT

NBA FINALS RECORD

MOST FINALS MVP AWARDS

Michael Jordan: 6

dominant play led the Houston Rockets to the 1994 and 1995 titles.

A new duo took over the NBA in the early 2000s. Massive center **Shaquille O'Neal** toyed with defenders under the hoop. Shooting guard **Kobe Bryant** torched them from the outside. The superstars didn't always get along off the court. But they thrived together on the court. The duo led the Los Angeles Lakers to a threepeat from 2000 to 2002. O'Neal soon left and won another championship with the Miami

Heat in 2006. Meanwhile, Bryant emerged from O'Neal's shadow. He played the starring role in back-to-back Lakers wins in 2009 and 2010.

Few teams could match up to those Lakers teams. But the San Antonio Spurs were one that did. The Spurs won four titles from 1999 to 2007. Then they added another in 2014. Power forward **Tim Duncan** led the way in all five. His play was rarely flashy. Instead, he simply did everything well. Mastering basic skills earned Duncan the nickname "Big Fundamental." He won three Finals MVP Awards.

SUPERSTAR WHISPERER

Phil Jackson won a pair of NBA titles as a player in the 1970s. But his coaching ability made him an icon. Jackson's thoughtful style and "triangle offense" set him apart. He also had a way of working with superstars such as Jordan and Bryant. In total, his Bulls and Lakers teams won 11 championships. No coach has won more titles.

DUNCAN
21

JAMES
6
HEAT
6

CHAPTER 3

MODERN GAME-CHANGERS

LeBron James entered the NBA with big expectations in 2003. By his fourth season, he led his hometown Cleveland Cavaliers to the NBA Finals. However, they fell to the Spurs. Still seeking a championship, James later moved to the Miami Heat. The Heat already had a superstar in **Dwyane Wade**. The athletic guard had won the Finals MVP Award in 2006.

Together, James and Wade led the Heat to four NBA Finals in a row. They won in 2012 and 2013. But James had much more to prove.

In 2014, he returned to Cleveland. By 2016, the Cavaliers were champions. James helped secure the city's first major championship in any sport in 52 years. Late in Game 7, he soared for a block to spark the upset win. The 2018 NBA Finals were James's eighth in a row. The streak ended the next year. But James joined the Los Angeles Lakers and won a fourth title in 2020. James earned the Finals MVP Award in all four of his titles.

The Golden State Warriors lost the 2016 Finals. But the team won in 2015, 2017, and 2018. Point guard **Steph Curry** shined as the sport's greatest three-point shooter. Forward

STAT SPOTLIGHT

NBA FINALS RECORD

THREE-POINTERS IN A GAME

Steph Curry: 9 (June 3, 2018)

Kevin Durant proved key to the latter two wins. His triple-double in Game 4 of the 2018 Finals helped the Warriors sweep the Cavaliers. Durant stuck around for one more season. Curry kept the team strong after that. In 2022, he led the Warriors to another title.

PROVEN WINNER

The Chicago Bulls needed a basket to secure the 1997 NBA title. They didn't call Michael Jordan's number. Instead, Steve Kerr hit the winning shot. The sharpshooting guard won five NBA titles as a player. In 2014–15, the Golden State Warriors hired Kerr as coach. By 2022, he had led the team to four titles.

A veteran core had turned the San Antonio Spurs into a power. However, a young forward broke out in their 2013 NBA Finals loss. The next year, **Kawhi Leonard** took over. He showed promising skills on offense. But his elite defense earned him Finals MVP and helped the Spurs win another championship. Before the 2018–19 season, the Toronto Raptors traded for Leonard. By then, Leonard was one of the league's best players. He spent only one season with Toronto. But he made the most of it. Leonard led the Raptors to their first NBA title.

The Milwaukee Bucks hadn't enjoyed much success after winning the title in 1971. Then **Giannis Antetokounmpo** developed into one of the league's biggest stars. The forward could take over a game with his freak athleticism. And that's just what he did in the 2021 Finals. Antetokounmpo averaged more than 35 points and 13 rebounds per game. Then in Game 6, his 50 points and 14 rebounds lifted Milwaukee to its second championship.

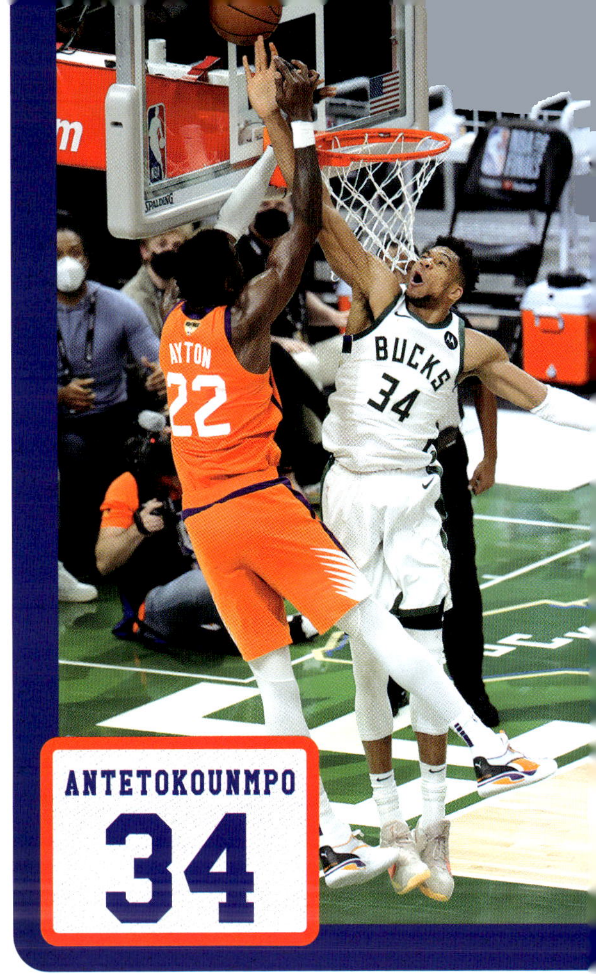

TIMELINE

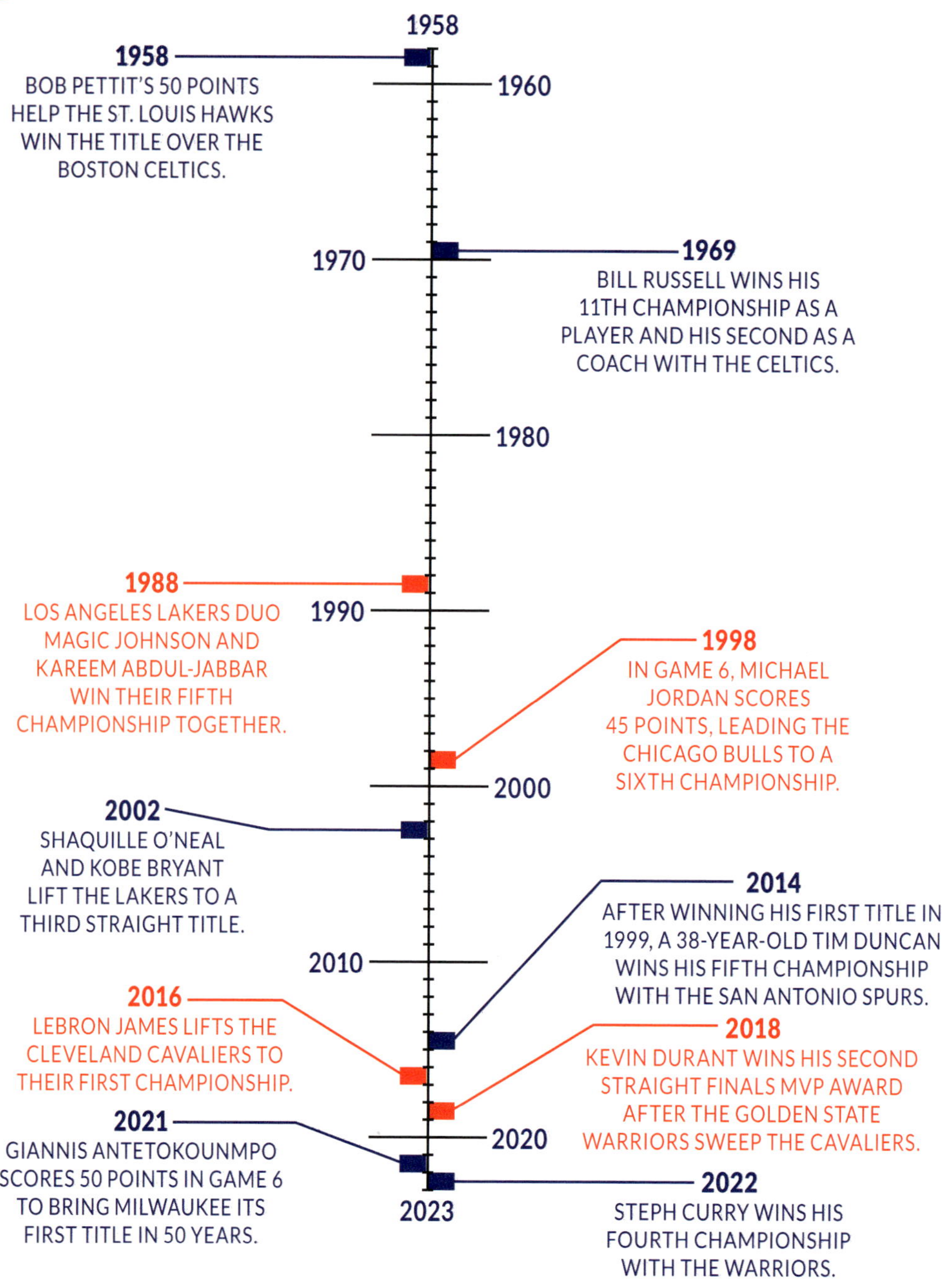

1958
BOB PETTIT'S 50 POINTS HELP THE ST. LOUIS HAWKS WIN THE TITLE OVER THE BOSTON CELTICS.

1969
BILL RUSSELL WINS HIS 11TH CHAMPIONSHIP AS A PLAYER AND HIS SECOND AS A COACH WITH THE CELTICS.

1988
LOS ANGELES LAKERS DUO MAGIC JOHNSON AND KAREEM ABDUL-JABBAR WIN THEIR FIFTH CHAMPIONSHIP TOGETHER.

1998
IN GAME 6, MICHAEL JORDAN SCORES 45 POINTS, LEADING THE CHICAGO BULLS TO A SIXTH CHAMPIONSHIP.

2002
SHAQUILLE O'NEAL AND KOBE BRYANT LIFT THE LAKERS TO A THIRD STRAIGHT TITLE.

2014
AFTER WINNING HIS FIRST TITLE IN 1999, A 38-YEAR-OLD TIM DUNCAN WINS HIS FIFTH CHAMPIONSHIP WITH THE SAN ANTONIO SPURS.

2016
LEBRON JAMES LIFTS THE CLEVELAND CAVALIERS TO THEIR FIRST CHAMPIONSHIP.

2018
KEVIN DURANT WINS HIS SECOND STRAIGHT FINALS MVP AWARD AFTER THE GOLDEN STATE WARRIORS SWEEP THE CAVALIERS.

2021
GIANNIS ANTETOKOUNMPO SCORES 50 POINTS IN GAME 6 TO BRING MILWAUKEE ITS FIRST TITLE IN 50 YEARS.

2022
STEPH CURRY WINS HIS FOURTH CHAMPIONSHIP WITH THE WARRIORS.

CHAMPIONSHIP FACTS

NBA FINALS

First played: 1947

Most titles as a player: Bill Russell, 11

Most titles as a coach: Phil Jackson, 11

Most titles by a team: Boston Celtics and Los Angeles Lakers, 17

Stats are accurate through the 2022–23 season.

MORE INFORMATION

To learn more about the NBA Finals, go to **pressboxbooks.com/AllAccess**.

These links are routinely monitored and updated to provide the most current information available.

GLOSSARY

dynasty
A team that has an extended period of success, usually winning multiple championships in the process.

icon
A person who is very famous or well known.

post
The area around the basket where power forwards and centers usually play.

sweep
To win all the games in a series.

swingman
A player who can play both guard and forward.

threepeat
When a team wins three championships in a row.

triple-double
When a player reaches 10 or more of three different statistics in one game.

upset
When a weaker team or player unexpectedly wins.

versatile
Able to do many different things.

veteran
A player who has spent several years in a league.

INDEX